Why Science Matters

Reducing Pollution

John Coad

www.heinemann.co.uk/library
Visit our website to find out more information about **Heinemann Library** books.

To order:
 Phone 44 (0) 1865 888066
 Send a fax to 44 (0) 1865 314091
 Visit the Heinemann Bookshop at www.heinemann.co.uk/library to browse our catalogue and order online.

Heinemann Library is an imprint of Capstone Global Library Limited, a company incorporated in England and Wales having its registered office at 7 Pilgrim Street, London, EC4V 6LB – Registered company number: 6695582

"Heinemann" is a registered trademark of Pearson Education Limited, under licence to Capstone Global Library Limited

Edited by Pollyanna Poulter and Rebecca Vickers
Designed by Steven Mead and Q2A Creative Solutions
Original illustrations © Capstone Global Library Limited by Gordon Hurden and International Mapping
Picture research by Ruth Blair
Production by Victoria Fitzgerald
Originated by Heinemann Library
Printed and bound in China by Leo Paper Group.

ISBN 978 0 431040 94 3 (hardback)
13 12 11 10 09
10 9 8 7 6 5 4 3 2 1

British Library Cataloguing-in-Publication Data
Coad, John
Reducing pollution. - (Why science matters)
1. Pollution - Juvenile literature 2. Pollution prevention - Juvenile literature
I. Title
363.7'37
A full catalogue record for this book is available from the British Library.

Acknowledgements
We would like to thank the following for permission to reproduce photographs: © Alamy pp. **7**, **9**, **12**, **14**, **24**, **28**, **29**, **30**, **44**; © AP Photos p. **47** (Lucy Pemoni); © Corbis pp. **4**, **5**, and **6** (Bettmann), **13** (Chase Jarvis), **15** (Sygma/Alain De Jean), **16** (Richard A. Cooke), **17** (Ted Spiegel), **18** (Sygma/Bernard Annebicque), **19** (Visions of America/Joseph Sohm), **21** (Sygma/Igor Kostin), **22** (epa/Uli Deck), **25** (NewSport/David Madison), **27** (Mark Peterson), **31** (George Steinmetz), **37** (Bojan Brecelj), **39** (BSPI), **40** (epa/Gerry Penny), **45** (KIPA/Gaudenti Sergio), © Ecoscene pp. **38**, **42**; © iStockphoto background images and design features, pp. **32** (Andrew Howe), (James Steidl), (Tomasz Zachariasz), (Xavier Marchant); © Photodisc p. **34** (Photolink/C. Lee); © Photolibrary p. **10** (Markus Renner); © Science Photo Library p. **41** (Emmeline Watkins).

Cover photograph of field drainage pipe with green outflow reproduced with permission of © Getty Images/Stockbyte.

We would like to thank Michael Mastrandrea for his invaluable help in the preparation of this book.

Every effort has been made to contact copyright holders of material reproduced in this book. Any omissions will be rectified in subsequent printings if notice is given to the Publishers.

Disclaimer
All the Internet addresses (URLs) given in this book were valid at the time of going to press. However, due to the dynamic nature of the Internet, some addresses may have changed, or sites may have changed or ceased to exist since publication. While the author and Publishers regret any inconvenience this may cause readers, no responsibility for any such changes can be accepted by either the author or the Publishers.

Contents

Some words are printed in bold, **like this**. You can find out what they mean in the glossary.

The bad old days

A river in flames!

In 1969, the Cuyohoga River that runs through Cleveland, Ohio, USA, caught fire. The fire was fuelled by industrial pollutants that had been discharged into the river. People believe that sparks from a train ignited an oil slick on the river. The fire lasted just 30 minutes but caused about US$50,000 worth of damage at the time, mainly to railway bridges crossing the river. The fire raised awareness of the state of the river. *Time* magazine wrote: *"Some river! Chocolate-brown, oily, bubbling with subsurface gases, it oozes rather than flows."*

The lower Cuyohoga had no visible signs of life that usually thrives on waste, not even low forms, such as leeches and sludge worms.

Pollution occurs when substances that can damage human health or harm **ecosystems** are released into the natural environment. Human activity has always created pollution through domestic and agricultural waste but the amount and range of pollution increased rapidly as countries became more **industrialized**. Initially there was very little concern for the environment and pollution was ignored. Eventually, however, people had to take notice.

London, UK, 5 December 1952

On the morning of 5 December, the weather in London was colder than usual. People burnt large amounts of coal, and smoke bellowed from chimneys. The winds were light and the air near the ground was moist – ideal conditions for the formation of fog. During the day the fog was not very dense, but at night it thickened and visibility dropped to a few metres. The fog was actually **smog**. It hung in the air for five days and worsened lung infections and breathing disorders, causing the premature death of over 4,000 people and making many ill.

The Seveso disaster

In July 1976, a valve broke at a chemical plant north of Milan in Italy. A cloud of chemicals rose high into the air and was carried by winds to the nearby community of Seveso. One of the chemicals released was dioxin, which is extremely **toxic** to humans. Within hours some children showed burn-like symptoms on their skin. Later, people developed chloracne, a severe skin disorder. Many animals died, and farm animals were slaughtered to prevent the poison being passed along the food chain. The most polluted area was evacuated and turned into a park. Both the Cuyohoga River and Seveso disasters led to greater regulation of industrial waste in the USA and Europe.

THE SCIENCE YOU LEARN: TEMPERATURE INVERSION

Normally, air closer to the ground is warmer than the air above it and, therefore, rises. Temperature inversions often happen on winter nights after the ground has cooled down so much that it begins to chill the air closest to it. This often causes mist to form as water vapour condenses on dust particles. Normally, the morning sun shines through the mist and heats the ground, which warms the air above it, breaking the inversion. In London in 1952, the mist close to the ground was so thick that the Sun never shone through, and the air stayed cool and static.

Who cares about pollution?

There have always been people who have cared about the environment. For example, in 1739 Benjamin Franklin, one of the founding fathers of the United States, campaigned against the dumping of waste in Philadelphia. However, it was after World War II in the 1950s and 1960s that people began to voice their concerns about pollution.

Following the protests at Amchitka island, Greenpeace was founded. It is now an international organization that campaigns to protect the marine environment.

The protest movement grows

In 1971 the U.S. Government planned to carry out underground nuclear tests near the tiny island of Amchitka, off the coast of Alaska. Endangered sea otters and rare birds lived on Amchitka and the proposed detonations sparked considerable protest. Some activists set off from Vancouver, Canada, sailing towards Amchitka in an old fishing boat. They didn't expect to stop the nuclear tests but did want to draw more media attention to them. They were successful – the testing went ahead but their protest increased public awareness. Before long nuclear testing was halted and Amchitka was declared a bird sanctuary.

The EU introduced new laws in 2007 to compel producers of electrical goods to pay for the recycling or safe disposal of old equipment.

Governments gain momentum

As more and more people became aware of environmental issues, governments began to act. In 1970, the U.S. Environmental Protection Agency (EPA) was created and the Clean Air Act was passed in 1972. That year the use of DDT was banned in the United States (see below).

In the United Kingdom, the discovery of dumped toxic waste in 1971 led to a public outcry and the first ever legislation to control toxic waste. It was the European Union (EU), however, that drove through legislation to protect the environment. A string of regulations have tackled pollution across Europe, backed up by threats of fines and even imprisonment.

CASE STUDY

Silent Spring

In 1962, American biologist Rachel Carson published a book called *Silent Spring*. The book described the effects of the wide-scale spraying of a **pesticide** called DDT (see also page 33). Carson argued that too little was known about the long-term effects of the pesticide on human health and other living systems. She suggested that DDT could cause cancer and was a real threat to wildlife, particularly birds.

Silent Spring was read and debated widely. Environmental interest grew and new pressure groups, such as Greenpeace and Friends of the Earth, were formed. Although some scientists still disagree with Carson there is no doubt that her book sparked a greater concern for what humans were doing to the environment.

Caring for the future

Pollution occurs in the air, at all levels of the atmosphere, and can affect human health and the climate. Oceans, rivers, **groundwater**, and the land can be damaged by pollutants. Pollution can be caused by a wide range of waste materials, by irresponsible use of chemicals, and through accidents.

Reducing pollution

Pollution occurs in different forms all around the world. There is no single way of tackling it. However, some types of pollution have been tackled successfully in some countries. This has been done by:

- individual people changing their habits
- groups of people raising awareness of problems
- governments passing and enforcing laws for their own country
- countries coming together to create international agreements.

This diagram has the most preferred way of dealing with waste at the top and the least preferred way at the bottom. Clearly it is best not to create waste in the first place.

REDUCE
Reduce waste or the need to recycle by not creating it in the first place.

REUSE
Reuse materials before recyling or discarding.

RECYCLE
Transform material into another usable material.

TREATMENT
Reduce volume or toxicity.

DISPOSAL
Store or bury waste.

Reduce, reuse, or recycle?

So how do we reduce pollution? Some people think that recycling is the answer and devote all their energy to that. Of course recycling is important, but there are better ways.

If everyone abandoned their cars and cycled we would solve the pollution problems caused by cars. But this is not a sustainable solution. The cost in travel time for long journeys (economics) and the problem of arriving sweaty and tired (social impact) means that we will not replace all cars with bikes.

Sustainable development

Tackling pollution requires us to act in a **sustainable** way. In the past, a common attitude was that nature exists for the convenience of humankind. In other words, humans could take and use any resources from Earth, disposing of waste with no concerns for the future. People also considered Earth to be so vast that their actions would not change it. We now know that this is not the case. Today, many more people understand that we should live responsibly so as not to use up Earth's natural wealth and create pollution.

Behaving in this way is described as sustainable living. Sustainability means that we should not consume more resources than our planet can provide, nor produce more waste than it can dispose of.

The role of scientists

When we think of sustainable development, environmental factors are the first to spring to mind. However, economic and social issues also need to be considered. It is no good finding a solution to an environmental problem that is expensive or has a negative impact on people's lives. Most people would not accept it and therefore it would not be sustainable.

New technologies are essential if we are to maintain our standard of living and have more sustainable lifestyles. Scientists play an important role in developing these technological solutions, for example finding ways of using **renewable** materials that avoid pollution. It is up to politicians, industry, and the public to then use these new technologies in a practical way.

The climate change threat

For hundreds of years we have relied on **fossil fuels** for our energy. Coal was used to power the industrial revolution. Now oil and gas are used for transport, heating, and electricity generation.

Using fossil fuels is not sustainable. They took millions of years to form and are being used up much faster than they can ever be formed. They will eventually run out. However, there is another reason for their use to be considered unsustainable. Very good scientific evidence indicates that burning fossil fuels is causing climate change.

Burning fossil fuels produces carbon dioxide. Many years ago, carbon dioxide would not have been considered a pollutant as it occurs naturally. However, the amount of carbon dioxide in the air is greater now than at any time in at least the past 500,000 years, and it is rising at an exceptionally high rate. Carbon dioxide is certainly a pollutant and it intensifies the greenhouse effect (see page 11), which is causing our planet to warm up.

As global temperatures climb, polar ice caps are crumbling and glaciers are melting. Since 1960, glaciers around the world have lost an estimated 8,000 km³ (1,900 miles³) of ice. This is evidence of climate change.

Evidence of climate change

- Temperatures around the world have increased by between 0.6 and 0.9°C (1.1 and 1.62°F) in the past 100 years
- There are more examples of extreme weather with record-breaking temperatures, floods, droughts, and violent storms
- Some species are shifting locations or migrating earlier
- Ice in the Arctic and Antarctic regions is melting
- Coral reefs are dying due to increased water temperatures.

The greenhouse effect

In a greenhouse the temperature inside is higher than outside. Why is this? Energy from the Sun passes through the glass and warms up the inside. However, the glass prevents heat energy from escaping. It is trapped so the greenhouse stays warm.

A number of gases in our atmosphere cause a similar effect around Earth. Without any greenhouse effect it is estimated that the average temperature on Earth would be −19°C (−2.2°F) rather than the 15°C (59°F) we enjoy. So, a natural greenhouse effect is essential for life on Earth. However, increasing **greenhouse gas** concentrations are now intensifiying the effect, causing temperatures to rise. Natural ecosystems and human society are threatened as global warming worsens.

The diagram shows how the greenhouse effect works.

2. Some radiation is reflected by Earth and the atmosphere.

3. Most radiation is absorbed by, and warms, Earth.

4. The warm Earth emits lower energy radiation. Greenhouse gas molecules absorb some of this. Less heat escapes and Earth's temperature rises.

1. High energy radiation from the Sun passes through the atmosphere.

THE SCIENCE YOU LEARN: GREENHOUSE GASES

There are a number of pollutant gases that contribute to the greenhouse effect. All these gases absorb **infrared** radiation emitted by the warm Earth and trap it in the atmosphere.

Gas	Formula	Relative effect
Carbon dioxide	CO_2	1
Methane	CH_4	21
Nitrous oxide	N_2O	300
Chlorofluorocarbons	Various, for example CCl_2F_2	2,000–12,000

Chlorofluorocarbons (CFCs, see page 40) are most effective at absorbing heat but the amount of them in the atmosphere is small and decreasing thanks to global co-operation on reducing their use. Carbon dioxide, while less effective than other pollutants, is being produced in much larger quantities by the burning of fossil fuels.

Reducing carbon footprints

To tackle climate change effectively both governments and individuals must work together. As individuals almost everything we do leads to emissions of carbon dioxide into the atmosphere. Most of our electricity is generated by burning fossil fuels, which release carbon dioxide. Our transport systems do the same. This means that whenever we use electrical appliances or travel we are responsible for greenhouse gas production. The amount of carbon dioxide your activities produce is known as your **carbon footprint**. This is because it suggests something that we leave behind for generations to come.

We are now encouraged to reduce our own carbon footprint. We can do this at home or at work by:

- turning off lights and electrical appliances, making sure that nothing is left on standby
- turning central heating and hot water temperature down slightly
- fitting energy-saving light bulbs
- insulating our homes and offices
- walking to school and work or sharing a car
- buying products (for example, fruit and vegetables) that have been grown or made close to home
- recycling as much as possible.

A British Government minister revealed that Britons waste the equivalent of about two power stations' worth of energy each year by leaving television sets and other gadgets on standby. Should Governments ban standby buttons? What do you think?

CUTTING EDGE: BURY THE CARBON

In April 2008, Australia began pumping carbon dioxide into empty natural gas reservoirs 2 km (1.2 miles) underground. This is just a trial project and the carbon dioxide will be monitored carefully to see if any escapes.

If the project is a success, carbon dioxide produced at power stations from burning coal and oil could be pumped to underground stores. Opponents of the scheme say this is not the best way to tackle climate change and the Australian government should be investing more in alternative technology.

Wind power is an alternative form of energy that does not produce carbon dioxide. However, wind alone cannot currently supply enough energy to replace fossil fuels. Some scientists believe that nuclear power (see page 20) is the best option for the future.

Government action

Some governments are already taking action. They have set tough targets for reducing carbon dioxide emissions and taken unpopular steps, such as taxing the most polluting cars and air flights. They are investing in forms of energy that do not use fossil fuels and working to prevent **deforestation** in tropical countries.

Worldwide agreement

In 1997, in the Japanese city of Kyoto, governments came together to tackle the problem of global warming. A treaty was signed that required 36 more economically developed countries to reduce their greenhouse gas emissions. The United States refused to be bound by the treaty, believing that new technologies, not cuts, were the best solution. While many people were sceptical of the value and possible impact of the agreement, it did provide hope that the world can act collectively to safeguard Earth's future. International conferences since then have tightened the emissions targets for some countries and agreed on ways of protecting vital forests.

The demand for energy

Our world runs on energy. The problem is that obtaining energy almost inevitably causes some form of pollution.

Dig it up and dump the waste

Coal is a fossil fuel that has been used for hundreds of years. In the past coal was mined with little concern for the environment. Waste from the mining process was piled in huge **slag heaps**, which contain chemicals that are washed out by rainwater, leading to river pollution.

In Alberta, Canada, there are huge deposits of tar sands. Here the oil is not runny enough to be pumped straight from the ground. Some near the surface is simply dug out and then processed to separate the tar from sand, soil, and water. For deeper deposits, high pressure steam is used. It takes about 2 tonnes of mined tar sands to get a 160-litre (42-gallon) barrel of oil. Thus huge amounts of waste are left over.

In Northern Alberta, Canada, the tar sands mining operations have clear-cut thousands of hectares of trees. The region is dotted with large human-made lakes filled with leftover waste from the mining operations.

CASE STUDY

Aberfan disaster

In October 1966, following days of heavy rain, a huge slag heap from a coal mine in South Wales became unstable and slipped down the mountainside. It destroyed 20 houses and a farm before engulfing the local junior school. A total of 144 people were killed, including 116 school children and 5 teachers. Although there was evidence that the heap had not been maintained properly and was known to be dangerous, no one was charged with negligence.

Transporting oil

Crude oil has to be transported from where it is extracted to oil refineries. Much of it is moved in huge ships called supertankers. Moving vast amounts of oil can be risky and there have been many examples of accidents and oil spills.

When the *Amoco Cadiz* lost control of its rudder, a tugboat tried to pull it to safety. The attempt failed, due to the huge mass of the ship and very strong winds.

The Amoco Cadiz

The world's worst spillage from a supertanker occurred in France in 1978. The *Amoco Cadiz* ran aground off the coast of Brittany and split in two, spilling 223,530 tonnes of crude oil. Strong winds smeared an oil slick 29 km (18 miles) wide and 128 km (80 miles) long down the coast. This led to a huge loss of marine life and nearly 20,000 birds were killed. Twenty years later, animal populations still showed the effects of the pollution while researchers estimated it would take decades for the ecosystem to return to its pre-spill levels.

Treating oil spills

Once an oil spill has occurred, many agencies work together to clean it up and minimize the damage to the environment. A number of techniques can be used. The simplest method is to burn the oil. This can remove over 95 percent of the spillage but produces a lot of smoke. Alternatively, booms floating on the surface of water are used to surround and contain the oil. It can then be sucked up by machines rather like large vacuum cleaners. Some materials, such as straw, will soak up the oil. Once the oil is washed ashore, detergents have to be used to break it up into tiny droplets and disperse it. Scientists are also studying some types of bacteria that they hope can be used to "eat" oil.

Air pollution – acid rain

Power stations, factories, and cars all burn fuels and, therefore, all produce polluting gases. Some of these gases (especially nitrogen oxides and sulfur dioxide) react with the tiny droplets of water in clouds to form sulfuric and nitric acids. The rain from these clouds then falls as a weak acid, which is known as **acid rain**.

Acid rain causes a lot of damage. It attacks buildings, particularly those made from limestone and marble. In large areas of Europe and North America millions of fir trees were killed by acid rain. The reasons for this are complex, but it seems that acid rain washes valuable minerals from the soil, releases harmful ones, and removes the waxy coating from leaves preventing them from **photosynthesizing** normally. Where acid rain runs into streams and rivers, fish are killed. Freshwater fish are very susceptible to changes in **pH** (acidity and alkalinity) and some lakes have had all animals and plants killed.

Scandinavian and Canadian forests have been badly affected by acid rain. But these countries did not produce the pollution, it was blown by winds from neighbouring countries.

One solution for tackling acid rain is to neutralize the acid in lakes with powdered limestone. This is called liming. Norway and Sweden have successfully used liming to help restore lakes and streams and a major liming programme is currently taking place in Wales, UK.

Prevention better than cure

Rather than tackling pollution, there are a number of ways to prevent it:

- Coal and oil contain impurities of sulfur. When the fuel burns, the sulfur also burns, forming sulfur dioxide. Many oil refineries now have a desulfurization process to remove the sulfur.
- Some power stations that burn coal have been fitted with "scrubbers" to treat the waste gases. The scrubbers spray a mixture of water and powdered limestone into the chimney. Legislation in the United States and Europe has influenced many coal-fired power stations to install scrubbers.
- Cars have been fitted with catalytic converters (see page 26). Although these do produce carbon dioxide, they also stop the formation of oxides of nitrogen.

THE SCIENCE YOU LEARN: THE pH SCALE

Acidity is measured using the pH scale. This scale ranges from zero to 14. Zero is the most acidic and 14 is the most alkaline (opposite of acidic). Something with a pH value of seven is neutral, neither acidic nor alkaline.

Carbon dioxide in the air dissolves in rainwater making it slightly acidic. Unpolluted rain therefore has a pH value between five and six. When the air becomes more polluted with nitrogen oxides and sulfur dioxide, the acidity can increase to a pH value of four. Some rain has even been recorded as being pH two.

The opposite of an acid is a base. If bases dissolve in water they make alkalis with a pH greater than seven. When a base is added to an acid a neutralization reaction occurs.

Limestone contains calcium carbonate, a common base. It will not dissolve in water but reacts readily with acids in rain.

INVESTIGATION: LICHEN BIOINDICATORS

Lichens are very simple organisms that grow on a variety of surfaces. They are two-part organisms made from an alga and a fungus. Although they are partners, the alga can live separately, but the fungus cannot. The alga produces food by photosynthesis for the fungus.

A simple investigation into air pollution can be carried out with samples of lichens. They can be obtained from biological suppliers or they can be found on twigs, sticks, or rocks. Information on the Internet will help you to identify any lichens found locally.

1. Take two or three different lichens. Create two samples of each and keep them in their own glass jar.
2. Prepare two spray bottles: one with pure water; the other with diluted vinegar, a weak acid.

3. Spray one set of lichens each day with a fine mist of the pure water. These are your control samples. Wearing safety goggles, spray the other set of lichens with the diluted vinegar. After spraying each sample cover it with clingfilm.
4. After several days, examine the lichens carefully. Does one set of lichens look less healthy than the other set?

Once we know which lichens are affected by weak acid, it is possible to measure where pollution occurs. Look for these lichens in places where you might expect pollution, such as near roads and factories. Compare these places with parks and gardens. Do you find more lichens in some places? This suggests these places are less polluted with acid rain.

Some lichens are good **bioindicators,** living things that can tell us how healthy an environment is by showing whether it is polluted.

Warm water discharged from power stations has less oxygen dissolved in it than cold river water. The difference can be enough to kill fish.

Thermal pollution

Power stations generating our electricity can cause another form of pollution – thermal (or waste heat) pollution. Many power stations are built near rivers because they need large amounts of water. Power stations always produce heat – from burning fossil fuels or from nuclear reactions. The heat produced turns water into steam, which drives the generators. Huge cooling towers allow most of the steam to condense back to water. However, the water does not cool completely and often it is discharged into rivers at a higher temperature than the river itself.

Sudden changes in water temperature can kill fish directly. The reduction in oxygen content can be fatal. One power station in California, USA, developed a "fish chase" procedure to reduce deaths. When hot water has to be discharged it is done gradually at first to drive the fish away from the area before the temperature reaches lethal levels.

 ## THE SCIENCE YOU LEARN: DISSOLVED OXYGEN

Air dissolves slightly in water. Fish and amphibians have gills that can take dissolved oxygen from the water. If there is no dissolved oxygen in the water, fish will die.

When you warm water the temperature doesn't have to rise much before you start to see little bubbles forming. This is some of the air that was dissolved. Raising the temperature reduces its solubility.

Nuclear power

Uranium is the chemical element used for nuclear power. In one of the most remarkable natural events, a slow moving neutron can be captured by a uranium nucleus, leading to the nucleus becoming unstable. That means the nucleus then splits into two smaller atoms and releases energy and more neutrons. A single atom splitting (called fission) can yield over 200 million times the energy of the neutron that triggered it. The energy released is used to convert water to steam, which then drives the turbines to generate electricity.

This process occurs in a nuclear reactor. As fast neutrons will not be captured, neutrons must be slowed down to increase the chance of their capture. A material known as a **moderator** does this. Also, as the fission reaction produces more neutrons than are used, some of them must be removed. If this was not done, a chain reaction could occur leading to an explosion. Control rods that can be inserted or withdrawn from the reactor absorb neutrons, reducing the rate of the process.

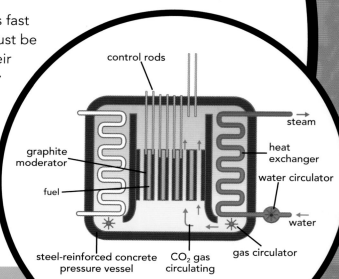

control rods

steam

heat exchanger

water circulator

graphite moderator

water

fuel

gas circulator

steel-reinforced concrete pressure vessel

CO_2 gas circulating

THE SCIENCE YOU LEARN: ENERGY FROM ATOMS

Every substance is made from tiny particles called atoms. But atoms themselves are made from even tinier particles called protons, neutrons, and electrons. Protons and neutrons are clumped together in the central part of an atom, called the nucleus. Some large atoms have a nucleus that can break apart. Substances whose atoms break in this way are said to be **radioactive**. They give out energy, break into smaller atoms, and emit electrons or neutrons. This splitting of atoms is called **nuclear fission**.

In a gas-cooled reactor, carbon dioxide gas cools the fuel and transfers the heat to the boilers. Control rods, when dropped down, stop the process completely. Graphite is the moderator used to slow down the neutrons.

The Chernobyl disaster

In the early hours of 26 April 1986, one of four nuclear reactors exploded at the Chernobyl power station in the Ukraine. Engineers testing the reactor had disabled safety systems and removed too many control rods from the nuclear core. The reactor began to overheat. With power at 100 times the normal, fuel pellets exploded and ruptured the fuel channels. Eventually, two huge explosions caused the reactor's dome-shaped roof to be blown off and the contents to erupt outwards. A fire burned for nine days.

The devastation at Chernobyl reinforces some opinions that nuclear power is too risky. Others claim that modern reactors are much safer and a similar disaster could not happen.

The explosions were only the beginning of the problem. The disaster released at least 100 times more radiation than the atom bomb dropped on Hiroshima, Japan, in World War II. Winds carried the waste over a wide area of Europe and traces of radioactive deposits were found in nearly every country in the northern hemisphere. Scandinavia was badly affected and there are still farms in the United Kingdom where sheep eating grass growing on contaminated land have to be regularly monitored.

Much of the fallout was deposited close to Chernobyl, in parts of Belarus, Ukraine, and Russia. More than 350,000 people moved away from these areas, but about 5.5 million remain. Incidences of cancer have increased in the area, but scientists have been surprised by the dramatic revival of wildlife. Scientists are wary, however. Some trees show signs of abnormal growth and genetic mutations have been seen in birds.

The reactor is now encased in a huge, concrete coffin, with another structure planned to cover the site to contain the radiation for the next 100 years.

Nuclear waste

The trouble with nuclear power is that it creates radioactive waste. This produces dangerous radiation, gives off heat, and can be chemically reactive. Radioactive waste is classified into three types, depending on how concentrated and dangerous it is.

- Low-level waste – includes things that have been in contact with radioactive material, such as old tools that have been discarded, protective equipment, clothing, and paper towels. It is compressed into blocks and stacked in containers, which will eventually be buried.
- Intermediate-level waste – mainly arises from the dismantling and reprocessing of spent fuel (fuel that can no longer be used). This goes into steel drums, which are then filled with concrete.
- High-level waste – material that has been in the reactor core itself. While this is only a small proportion of all radioactive waste it contains 95 percent of the radioactivity. It is transported to a special plant where it is chopped up and boiled in acid until it dissolves. The mixture that is left is heated to over 1,000°C (1,830°F) and mixed with glass beads, before being cooled in special containers ready for storage.

THE SCIENCE YOU LEARN: RADIOACTIVE HALF-LIFE

Different radioactive materials decay, emitting radiation, at different rates. The one thing they have in common is that the more of the substance there is, the faster it decays. This makes it impossible to say exactly when all the atoms in a sample of a substance will have decayed. Scientists therefore use the idea of half-life. The half-life of a substance is the time it takes for half the sample to decay. Some substances have very short half-lives, others take thousands, even millions, of years. These substances are the most difficult to dispose of.

Many people understand the need for nuclear power, but still would not want even low-level waste, like this, stored near their homes.

Waste disposal

Scientists have considered several ways of disposing of nuclear waste, including firing it into space. However, the options with the least risk are:

- put it deep underground and make it as safe as possible
- keep storing it at or near the surface for a long time in the hope that new treatment technologies will be developed.

Neither option is popular with the public. People do not want nuclear waste stored near their homes, especially as some high-level waste has a half-life of millions of years. Some arguments for and against the two options are listed in the table below.

DEEP UNDERGROUND DISPOSAL	
Advantages	**Disadvantages**
• The decision is made, so less for future generations to worry about • May be more safe and secure as waste is deep underground and sealed off	• Needs particular rock formations that are only found in some areas, and the rock must be very strong to prevent the waste from ever escaping • Waste must be well away from any watercourses, so not to contaminate water supplies • Excavation would be difficult and expensive, making it hard for future generations to manage the waste differently
LONG-TERM SURFACE STORAGE	
Advantages	**Disadvantages**
• Waste is retrievable, accessible, and easy to monitor • Could be kept at nuclear sites where waste is produced so no need for transport • Less expensive in the short-term	• Future generations are faced with the problem of surface waste • Large-scale costs in the long term • May be less safe and secure from possible terrorist attacks or natural disasters

Should we or shouldn't we?

Arguments rage on about nuclear power. Many scientists and governments believe it is the only way to generate enough electricity and reduce our dependence on fossil fuels. Opponents argue that generating waste which we cannot dispose of safely is wrong and that we are storing up problems for the future.

Transport

Cars and emissions

If car engines were to burn petrol efficiently, the only substances emerging in the exhaust would be carbon dioxide and water vapour. Unfortunately, other chemical reactions also occur in the engine. These reactions produce pollutants, released in a car's exhaust.

- In the confined space of a car's engine there is not enough oxygen for all the fuel to burn completely. This leads to pollutants of carbon monoxide, fine soot particles, and perhaps some unburned fuel.
- A spark in the car's engine ignites the fuel. This causes some nitrogen in the air to combine with oxygen, making oxides of nitrogen. These nitrogen oxide pollutants dissolve in rainwater to make acids.
- Sunlight acts on pollutants to produce **ozone**. This is a vital gas in the upper atmosphere, but is harmful at ground level.

These pollutants are all harmful individually, but together they contribute to the smog that affects many major cities.

The geography, weather, and reliance on motor vehicles makes Los Angeles one of the most polluted cities in the USA. Efforts have been made to improve the air quality, and the number of smog alerts has dropped from 100 per year in the 1970s to almost zero now.

CUTTING EDGE: REDUCE POLLUTION, REDUCE CRIME

For many years a compound of lead was added to petrol to make a more efficient fuel. Inevitably, fine particles of lead compounds were emitted from exhaust pipes. Lead is toxic and causes a loss of intelligence and disruption of behaviour to people in contact with it. In the 1970s, levels of lead near many busy roads were found to be above the safe limit. There was evidence that some children in urban areas were being harmed by lead poisoning.

By making small changes to engines and the fuel, oil companies were able to eliminate lead. The change brought about a 90 percent reduction in the average levels of lead in people's blood, and possibly an unexpected bonus. A 2007 report suggested that crime levels had fallen as a result. The science suggested that there was a strong link between the exposure of children to lead and their criminal behaviour as young adults. Countries that were the first to ban lead in petrol were the first to see reductions in crime.

The Beijing Olympic Games

For several years before the 2008 Olympic Games people — particularly long distance runners and cyclists — were worried about air pollution in China's capital city. In early 2008, Haile Gebrselassie of Ethiopia, one of the world's top marathon runners, announced that he would not compete in the Beijing marathon as he feared pollution could damage his health.

According to data obtained from the European Space Agency's satellites, air pollution in Beijing had increased by 50 percent from 1995 to 2005. The World Bank warned that China has 16 of the world's 20 most polluted cities; in Beijing air pollution was blamed for more than 400,000 premature deaths per year. Why has the pollution worsened so dramatically? The answer is simple — an explosion in car ownership. From just over one million cars on Beijing's streets at the turn of this century, it is estimated that there were three million by the start of the Olympics.

Chinese government officials promised clean air for the games. The country switched from coal to gas energy, planted millions of trees, closed down or moved a number of factories, and many old, heavily polluting cars were forced off the road. During the event air quality in Beijing did improve, but there were periods of smog.

Haile Gebrselassie holds the marathon world record and is a double Olympic gold medallist. He was the first high-profile athlete to pull out of a Beijing Olympic 2008 event over air pollution fears.

Catalytic converters

In many countries governments have passed laws restricting the amounts of pollutants a vehicle can produce. Manufacturers have improved car engines and fuel systems to keep within these laws. One of these improvements has been the development of catalytic converters. Their job is to turn harmful pollutants into less harmful gases before they leave the car's exhaust system.

A catalytic converter consists of a cylindrical body filled with a honeycomb structure made of ceramic material. This has been coated with the **catalyst** – a mixture of platinum, palladium, and rhodium metals. The honeycomb structure creates a huge surface area (equivalent to two football pitches) inside a relatively small space.

Most modern cars are fitted with a three-way converter as part of their exhaust system. The name refers to the three types of emission they help to reduce.

A three-way catalytic converter.

gases from engine: nitrogen oxides, hydrocarbons, carbon monoxide

honeycomb structure coated with catalyst

exhaust gases: carbon dioxide, water vapour, nitrogen

- Primarily, the converter turns oxides of nitrogen back into harmless nitrogen and oxygen gases.
- Secondly, it oxidizes unburned hydrocarbons and carbon monoxide, forming just carbon dioxide and water.
- Finally, it has sensors to monitor the exhaust flow and adjust fuel and air intake for greater fuel efficiency.

When lead was added to petrol, catalytic converters could not be used. The lead would "poison" the catalyst, preventing it from working. Eliminating lead from petrol was, therefore, doubly important in reducing pollution.

Authorities claim that aircraft are quieter now and the problem of noise is less severe. Residents disagree – while individual planes are quieter, there are many more of them.

Noise annoys

Heathrow airport in London is one of the busiest international airports in the world. The aircraft arriving and departing use vast amounts of fuel. Burning fuel creates greenhouse gases and pollutants, such as nitrogen oxides, creating air pollution. However, there is another form of pollution that bothers people living close to the airport – noise.

Depending on the wind direction, many planes fly in over central London. The first arrivals begin early in the morning. Many residents that live near flight paths are woken up by the noise they make. With the daily arrival of hundreds of flights, this noise is repeated countless times through the day.

The UK government claims that an average noise of 57 decibels (dB) or above throughout the day marks the start of community annoyance. They even publish maps showing the areas that are affected by such noise levels. Individual aircraft taking off create much more noise. This is monitored by sensors about 6.5 km (4 miles) from take off. During the day the noise must not exceed 94 dB and at night, 87 dB. Fines are imposed on aircraft that break these limits.

 THE SCIENCE YOU LEARN: MEASURING SOUND

Noise levels are measured in dB, the decibel scale that reflects the sensitivity of human ears to different levels of sound.
- 40 dB is a quiet sitting room, without anyone in it speaking
- 80 dB is shouting
- 100 dB is the limit that most manufacturers set for audios with earphones
- 130 dB is an aeroplane taking off 100 m (328 ft) away
- 140 dB is the level at which noise is painful to listen to for most people

Prolonged exposure to sounds over 80 dB can damage your ears.

Agricultural pollution

Plants use photosynthesis to make their own food from carbon dioxide and water. They also need some minerals, which are absorbed from the soil through their roots.

- Nitrogen is essential for the production of plant proteins and chlorophyll (which gives leaves their green colouring and helps plants absorb light)
- Phosphorus is needed for healthy flower and seed growth
- Potassium helps plants produce proteins and good fruit production.

When plants die and decay, the **nutrients** are returned to the soil for the next generation of plants to use. However, when farmers remove crops for food, the nutrients cannot be returned to the soil. Eventually plants will not grow there.

Nitram is a fertilizer that only contains ammonium nitrate. This is 35 percent nitrogen, but has no phosphorus or potassium. Nitram is used to boost the growth of crops, such as wheat.

Fertilizers

Fertilizers provide essential nutrients and are used extensively in farming, but they can cause pollution. When rain washes fertilizers off the soil into streams and lakes it can cause **eutrophication**. Fertilizers encourage the growth of green plants and algae in water. **Algae** turn the water green, which blocks off light to plants below the water surface. These plants die and bacteria feed on them as they decay. The bacteria use up oxygen in the water that is essential for fish and other creatures (see page 19). Eventually, normal life in the water dies out.

Many farmers store their animal manure, mixed with water, in a slurry tank. The slurry can be spread on fields as a fertilizer. Some of the worst cases of agricultural pollution have happened when slurry has been accidentally spilled into a river. Now there are strict regulations on where slurry tanks can be situated.

Fertilizer control

What can be done to reduce the pollution by fertilizers? One solution is to be more careful in the use of these chemicals. Farmers nowadays are much more aware of how to use fertilizers efficiently. They should not be spread during rainy weather and it is best to use them when plants are ready to take up the nutrients. Fertilizers that are slow to dissolve and release nutrients gradually might work well on some crops.

THE SCIENCE YOU LEARN: BIOLOGICAL OXYGEN DEMAND

Micro-organisms decompose any organic material – manure or sewage, for example – that enters a river or stream. These microbes use up oxygen in the water. This leads to the death of fish and possible eutrophication. The amount of oxygen that a litre of waste material uses up is called biological oxygen demand (BOD). Agricultural wastes have high BOD compared to domestic sewage.

Green fertilizers

Nitrogen is the most common gas in the atmosphere, but most plants are unable to use it in that form. A few plants, called legumes (for example, peas, beans, and clover), can directly use nitrogen gas. Many **organic** farmers will now grow a crop of peas or clover and plough it straight back into the soil. As the plants decay, the nitrogen is released for the following crop.

Other "green" fertilizers are compost and manure. Manure consists largely of animal dung. It contains the essential nutrients for plants, but it, too, can be washed off fields by rainwater. In waterways, it will decompose with the bacteria that lives on it using the dissolved oxygen in the water.

Lake Erie

In the 1960s, one of the five Great Lakes in North America was declared "dead". Ironically, it was full of life – just not the right kind. Eutrophication had claimed Lake Erie and excessive algae became the dominant plant species, killing off native aquatic species by soaking up all of the oxygen.

Lake Erie is the shallowest and warmest of the Great Lakes. Nearby land is intensively developed with agriculture, urban areas, industries, and sewage treatment plants. For decades, pollution filled Lake Erie with far more nutrients than the lake could handle. Plants began growing, dying, and decomposing in Lake Erie. This led to a severe deficiency of oxygen at the bottom of the lake and left the water's surface putrid and mossy. The lack of oxygen killed fish and other aquatic species, and the smelly surface repelled anglers, tourists, and those living near by.

The first step towards tackling the problem was to find the main cause. Scientists agreed that phosphorus was the key element and controlling this would reduce eutrophication. The phosphorus came from chemicals called phosphates (found in fertilizers and detergents).

In 1972, the United States and Canada signed an agreement to improve the water quality in the Great Lakes. Emphasis was placed on reducing the amount of phosphorus that was reaching them. Regulations were introduced to ensure phosphates were removed from detergents and waste water. Today, after years of hard work and co-operation, the phosphorus problem has essentially disappeared. Though the lake is much healthier, it has not yet recovered to its former natural state.

For environmentalists in North America, bringing Lake Erie "back to life" is just one indication that industries and communities can change to create a healthier, sustainable environment.

INVESTIGATION: MEASURING WATER POLLUTION

Complex instruments are needed to accurately identify and measure pollutant chemicals in streams and rivers. However, a simple way of judging pollution in a river is to look at the creatures living in it.

Find a stretch of river that is safe. It must be shallow, slow moving, and easily accessible. Only do this when accompanied by an adult. Using a small fishing net, take a sample from an area near the riverbank and, if possible, by some reeds. Tip the contents of the net into a white dish and identify any creatures in the sample. Next, carefully wade into a shallow part of the stream. Hold the net underwater, facing upstream, and move some stones on the bottom of the stream, in front of the net. Collect a sample of what has been disturbed. Again, empty the sample into a white dish and identify any creatures.

Some small creatures can live in water with little oxygen. Examples are blood worms, tubifex worms, or rat-tailed maggots. If this is all you find, the river is quite badly polluted. If you find stone-fly nymphs, mayfly nymphs, or freshwater shrimps then your river is much healthier with high levels of oxygen.

Other basic tests can easily be carried out using simple equipment. Measuring the temperature of a river in different places would identify any heat pollution. And a simple pH meter would show whether there is any acid or alkali contamination.

These students are investigating pollution by taking water samples from a river. The samples will be taken to the school chemistry lab for analysis.

Pesticides

Pests can destroy or damage crops. Farmers use chemicals called pesticides to control them. Pesticide is a broad term and includes products such as slug pellets and ant powder that you may use around your home and garden. Other pesticides you may have heard of include insect killers (insecticides), mould and fungi killers (fungicides), and weed killers (herbicides). Pesticides are poisons so are dangerous. They can harm humans, wildlife, and the environment. There are strict controls over their sale and – in most countries – farmers must be trained in their use.

Food chains and bioaccumulation

A food chain shows what eats what in a particular habitat. It shows the movement of energy in food from one organism to the next. Food chains almost always start with a green plant. These are called producers and use the Sun's energy to make food by photosynthesis. Animals that eat the plants, or each other, are called consumers. Below is an example of a food chain.

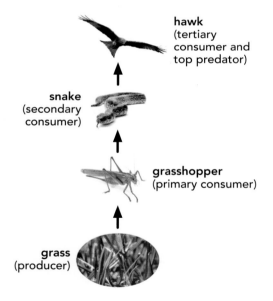

hawk
(tertiary consumer and top predator)

snake
(secondary consumer)

grasshopper
(primary consumer)

grass
(producer)

Farmers count on the level of pesticides used to control pests as being too low to harm humans. However, some pesticides stay in the body, building up in fatty tissue. As a result, pesticides can be passed along a food chain and accumulate in the top predator – **bioaccumulation**. Sometimes pesticide levels can be fatal.

CUTTING EDGE: REDUCING PESTICIDE POLLUTION

Instead of using chemical pesticides, natural predators can be used to destroy pests. For example, ladybirds and their larvae feed on aphids. Aphids, such as blackfly and greenfly, can damage a range of crops. Now, flightless ladybirds are bred and introduced to crops to eat aphids. These captive ladybirds are much more effective than regular ladybirds as they cannot fly away.

Another approach is to produce crops that are themselves resistant to pests. This involves **genetic modification.** One example is the cotton plant that has had a gene from a bacterium inserted into its **DNA** so it will produce a chemical toxic to its pests.

DDT

The pesticide DDT was the key subject of Rachel Carson's book *Silent Spring* (see page 7). DDT is an abbreviation for a long chemical name: dichloro-diphenyl-trichloroethane. It was first made in 1874, but not used as an insecticide until 1939. It was found to be very effective at controlling mosquitoes that spread malaria. After World War II, DDT was made available as an agricultural pesticide and its use rocketed.

In the late 1960s, pressure grew in the United States to ban DDT as many examples of environmental damage were observed. Fish were killed and populations of birds of prey, such as ospreys and bald eagles, declined significantly. DDT was shown to cause a thinning of egg shells, leading to thin and fragile eggs that hindered reproduction.

DDT was first banned in Norway and Sweden in 1970 and in the United States in 1972. It took until 1984 for a similar ban in the United Kingdom. However, DDT can still be used to control malaria in developing countries. Since the ban, osprey and eagle populations in the United States have greatly recovered.

A legacy of DDT use is that traces of it can be found practically all around the world. It has even been found in penguins in the Antarctic!

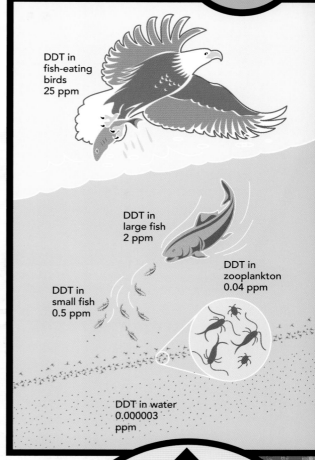

DDT in fish-eating birds 25 ppm

DDT in large fish 2 ppm

DDT in zooplankton 0.04 ppm

DDT in small fish 0.5 ppm

DDT in water 0.000003 ppm

DDT killed birds of prey and large fish because it was passed along the food chain and accumulated in the large animals, reaching toxic levels. PPM stands for "parts per million", that is the number of milligrams in one kilogram of the animal.

Detecting and identifying pollution

How do scientists monitor and detect sources of pollution? Imagine a small town where several dog owners have been to the vet. Their dogs are sick, but the vet is unable to work out why. Eventually, the vet discovers that all the dog owners regularly walked their dogs along the bank of the local river. The dogs often drink from the river so there could be something in the water. The vet sends samples of river water to the local water quality-testing laboratory.

Water analysis results

The lab runs a gas chromatography analysis of the river water that the dogs have been drinking. The results indicate the presence of an unknown substance. The scientists at the lab compare the results with data they have kept on file from other chromatography tests. If results match data gathered from passing a mixture of pesticides through the instrument, the scientists have identified the pollutant!

CASE STUDY

Gas chromatography

Scientists use a technique called gas chromatography to identify pollutants. A small sample is injected into the instrument where it is vaporized (converted into vapour). A gas pushes the sample through a long coil (known as the column), packed with non-reactive material. Some substances are carried through the coil quickly and others stick to the material. Thus, substances are separated in the coil. The time it takes each substance to pass through the coil indicates what the chemical is.

The column in a GC-MS machine is up to 30 m (98 ft) long, but only 0.25 mm (0.01 in) wide. The column is heated in a gas chromatograph to make sure the sample passing through the column stays as a gas.

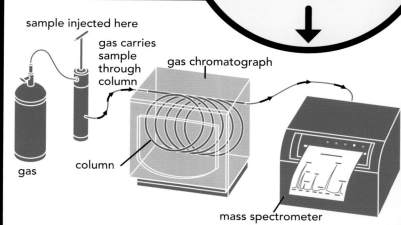

sample injected here

gas carries sample through column

gas chromatograph

gas

column

mass spectrometer

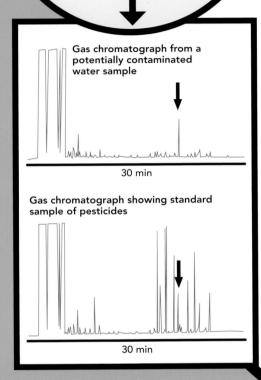

The top trace is the river water sample. The bottom trace is the standard sample of several pesticides. The matching peak on both traces is due to a pesticide called pentachlorophenol.

Gas chromatograph from a potentially contaminated water sample

30 min

Gas chromatograph showing standard sample of pesticides

30 min

Measuring pollutant levels

Scientists measure small amounts of pollutants using another instrument called a spectrophotometer. A chemical is added to the water sample that will combine with the pollutant to make a coloured substance. The colour will be much too pale to see with the naked eye, but the spectrophotometer will detect it. From the intensity of the colour, the pollutant concentration will be calculated.

Imagine that, in this case, pentachlorophenol is found to be the pollutant present at 5 ppb. The safe limit of pentachlorophenol is just 1 ppb, so the toxic pesticide pollutant is present at a level high enough to harm dogs and humans. Identifying the pollutant isn't enough. The scientists must determine whether it is present in large enough quantities to poison the dogs. Government scientists determine safe limits for hazardous chemicals. Usually, the maximum limits are measured in parts per million (ppm), or even parts per billion (ppb). If the pollution exceeds the permitted levels, then the health authorities will be contacted, and they will trace the polluter.

THE SCIENCE YOU LEARN: PARTS PER MILLION (PPM)

In the test tubes below, Tube A contains a 10 percent solution of food colouring – a 1 in 10 mixture. 1 cm³ is taken from Tube A and mixed with 9 cm³ of water in Tube B. This dilution is repeated to give the following mixtures:

A	B	C	D	E	F
	1cm³ A	1cm³ B	1cm³ C	1cm³ D	1cm³ E
	9 cm³ water	9 cm³ water	9 cm³ water	9 cm³ water	9 cm³ water
1 in 10	1 in 100	1 in 1,000	1 in 10,000	1 in 100,000	1 in 1 million

The colour is still in Tube E but can no longer be seen as it is so diluted. Tube F contains 1 part food colouring per million parts water. 1 ppm means 1 gram in a million, or 0.001 grams in 1,000 grams.

The chemical industry

There are many things that we take for granted nowadays that our ancestors didn't have, such as medicines, fertilizers, computers, and mobile phones. The chemical industry has been involved in the development and production of all these things. This industry is vital for our economy and to provide many materials and goods for our modern lifestyles. However, only a minority of people in the western world view the chemical industry favourably. Most have a negative image, influenced no doubt by a belief that chemicals are harmful and polluting.

In a European survey only 25 percent of people viewed the chemical industry favourably. Young people were the most negative. Is this point of view influenced by thoughts that the chemical industry is environmentally unfriendly?

Cleaning up its act

There is no doubt that the chemical industry has caused a great deal of pollution, such as in the Seveso disaster (see page 5). However, the chemical industry is now much cleaner and greener than it was. There are a number of reasons for this:

- Laws have been passed and regulations imposed to prevent pollution. Companies are inspected regularly and can be fined heavily if they fail to meet government standards.
- Companies are very concerned about their public image. Being identified as a major polluter is bad for a company and bad for business.

Unfortunately, the huge improvements made in many countries have not happened globally. In less economically developed countries regulations might not be so tight and strict laws are not always enforced.

Environmental health and safety specialist

Jennifer Watts is 28-years-old and works for a chemical company in the UK. The site at which she works manufactures chemicals for the **pharmaceutical** industry. Her role is focused mainly on environmental management at the site.

"I have to keep up to date with changing laws and regulations to ensure my site obeys all the rules. I routinely check and analyze air, water, and land emissions. Other responsibilities include staff environmental training and compiling records of waste disposed of. If anything goes wrong I am involved in investigating the incident and reporting on it. I am also responsible for maintaining our good relationships with the Environment Agency."

This environmental scientist is monitoring air quality on the roof of an industrial site. If pollutant limits are exceeded they must be reported to the authorities and investigated thoroughly.

Monitoring waste

Industry inevitably produces waste. Nowadays, industry is required to dispose of that waste responsibly. In Europe and the USA there are regulations governing the disposal of wastes and government bodies to check that industries comply.

- Emissions from chimneys must be monitored regularly. There are strict limits on the amounts of pollutant gases that can be emitted.
- Waste water cannot be run off into drains and sewers. Any pollutants must be removed before the water goes for treatment.
- When solid waste is taken away for dumping, the company must know where it is going and how it is disposed of.

No quick solution

We have seen how tougher laws and public expectation have led to reduced pollution from the chemical industry. However, even when laws are passed and chemicals are banned, the problems don't suddenly disappear.

Gender-changing pollutants

Some animals throughout the world are undergoing unnatural sexual changes as a result of environmental pollution, according to a group of scientists. Male animals have been found with female characteristics and vice versa. There is evidence that human-made chemicals cause these gender-changing effects, which could seriously threaten alligators, frogs, and other wildlife.

Persistent organic pollutants (POPs) are some of the chemicals blamed. POPs are hazardous and environmentally persistent substances. They can be transported between countries in oceans and the atmosphere. The substances are passed along food chains and have been traced in the fatty tissues of humans and animals.

Plasticizers

Chemicals are added to some plastics to make them soft and flexible. These chemicals are called plasticizers. They are particularly used with the plastic called polyvinyl chloride (PVC). It has long been known that plasticizers can move out of PVC and, as a result, have been extensively studied to see if they are harmful. Opinion is divided but, to be safe, three plasticizers have been banned from children's toys in Europe. Others have been restricted to toys that cannot be put in the mouth.

One scientific study showed that polar bears contain significant amounts of a POP used as a fire retardant on furniture and carpets. The bears were found to have 70 times as much of the POP as the seals they feed on. Some female bears also had male characteristics.

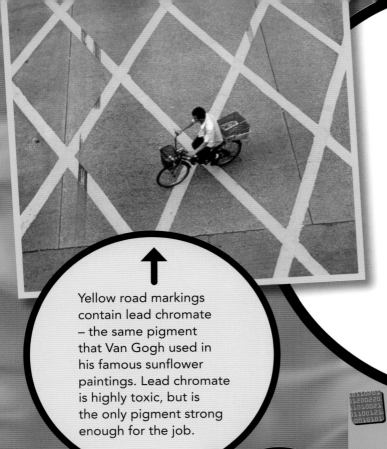

Yellow road markings contain lead chromate – the same pigment that Van Gogh used in his famous sunflower paintings. Lead chromate is highly toxic, but is the only pigment strong enough for the job.

Paints

Paints contain a number of substances. The most important is the pigment (coloured chemical). In the past, lead compounds were used as pigments. Lead compounds are particularly toxic. In 1978, the United States made it illegal to use any paint containing more than 0.06 percent lead for residential structures, hospitals, and children's products. However, it is still widely used on bridges, car parks, road signs, and other large-scale projects.

CASE STUDY

Lead paint on toys

Why use lead paint on toys? The answer is simple – the paint is hard-wearing, bright, fast-drying, and cheap. In 2007, the toy company Mattel found that a Chinese subcontractor had used lead paint from unauthorised suppliers on their products. Mattel had to recall hundreds of thousands of their toys from shops at a huge cost to the company.

CUTTING EDGE: PAINT THAT EATS POLLUTION

In 2004, a new paint was launched that absorbs pollutants from car exhausts. The paint has incredibly small particles of titanium dioxide and calcium carbonate embedded in it. The paint is porous enough to allow nitrogen oxide pollutants to pass into it. There they are absorbed by the titanium dioxide and calcium carbonate particles. The paint was trialled on the wall of a London school between 2005 and 2007. Pollution levels at the painted surface were reduced. However, 2.5 m (8 ft) away from the painted surface there seemed to be no effect. More tests are planned.

Another threat to the atmosphere

Early refrigerators used chemicals, such as ammonia, as refrigerants (cooling devices). If any chemicals escaped they could kill people. U.S. chemist Thomas Midgley (1889–1944) discovered replacement chemicals based on the elements carbon, fluorine, and chlorine. These were non-flammable and non-toxic – perfect for refrigerators – and became known as chlorofluorocarbons (CFCs). The CFCs were soon widely used and also proved to be valuable propellants in aerosol cans.

IN THE HOME: AEROSOLS

Look carefully at any aerosol cans you might have at home. In the past they would have contained CFCs as a propellant under pressure. It is this propellant that carries the deodorant, hairspray, or polish (for example) when the spray is released. CFCs have been banned and the propellant is now likely to be a gas called butane.

Old fridges must now be recycled carefully to ensure that any CFCs they contain cannot escape into the atmosphere. The number awaiting recycling has created "fridge mountains" in some countries.

Unfortunately, the chemicals were not as safe as first thought. Being particularly unreactive, they remained in the environment for a long time. They spread through the atmosphere and reacted with ozone. Ozone is a gas that occurs naturally in the upper atmosphere and absorbs much of the **ultraviolet** (UV) radiation that reaches us from the Sun. In parts of the world, particularly near the poles, the ozone layer has now thinned (partly due to the use of CFCs). A thinner ozone layer means higher levels of UV, which has resulted in increased incidences of skin cancer. An international treaty, signed in 1987, led to the phasing out of CFCs. Although the "ozone hole" over the Antarctic was the worst it has ever been in 2006, there are signs that it will recover in the next 50 years.

The painkiller ibuprofen was manufactured by six chemical reactions producing large amounts of waste. Green chemists redesigned the process to involve just three reactions, a re-usable catalyst, and less waste.

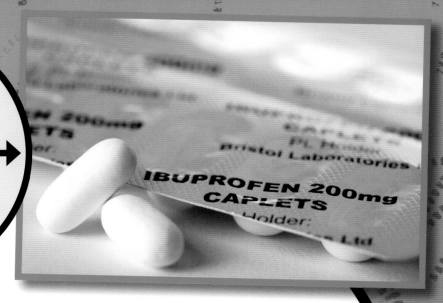

Green Chemistry

Many people think we need a new, more sustainable approach to using chemicals. This approach is called Green Chemistry. The principles of Green Chemistry include:

- design safer chemicals and processes
- avoid waste
- use renewable chemicals in all processes
- consider the whole life-span of the chemical – where it comes from and what will happen to it at the end of its life.

Many universities are now teaching Green Chemistry and exciting new environmentally-friendly chemicals are being produced.

CUTTING EDGE: RESHAPING CHEMISTRY

When someone has finished with an out-of-date laptop computer, what happens to the plastic casing? Chances are it ends up in a landfill. But what if the plastic was made from natural, **biodegradable** compounds? And what if, by introducing an **enzyme**, the plastic could be converted back to raw material, so a new laptop casing could be moulded from scratch? The process would produce less waste and less pollution. It would use less energy and it would reduce the need for petroleum – the basic ingredient of modern plastics, which is often extracted from fossil fuels.

This is the type of research being done in some universities as the Green Chemistry movement grows. Already, new biodegradable plastics, environmentally friendly pigments, and new medical treatments have been produced, while the use of hazardous solvents has been reduced.

Throw it away!

We live in a throw-away society. Anything we have finished with is usually thrown out for the refuse (rubbish) collector to take away. Few of us ever think or care about what happens next.

IN THE HOME: PACKAGING

Packaging accounts for half the refuse thrown away in some households. Not only are goods over-packaged, but we also increasingly tend to consume individual portions, which results in more waste. Buying coffee in individual pods, for instance, demands ten times more packaging than a 250 g (9 oz) jar.

Some people dispose of their refuse by the roadside. This is known as fly tipping. If we had to pay more for our refuse to be disposed of would more people resort to fly tipping?

Most refuse is dumped in landfill sites, buried, and left hidden. However, some of the refuse decomposes underground, releasing carbon dioxide and methane – both greenhouse gases. Rainwater soaks through landfill sites and can gradually wash a whole range of chemicals out of the decomposing waste. Some of these chemicals might have a high biological oxygen demand (BOD). This means that they use up a lot of dissolved oxygen. Waste with high BOD levels harms rivers that the rainwater soaks away to. Other chemicals from landfill sites might be toxic. Authorities have to monitor landfill sites for a long time after they have closed to check what is soaking away into the groundwater.

What are the alternatives?

In some places, refuse is **incinerated**. The heat produced can be used to drive generators to produce electricity. This makes sense but there are still risks. Incineration releases particulate matter and air pollutants, including carbon dioxide. Domestic refuse can also contain plastics, which release poisonous substances when burned. There is still a lot of debate about the safety of incinerators.

Sewage

There is some waste that we cannot avoid making, for example, every time we go to the toilet. Most people in more economically developed countries live with urban wastewater systems. Large pipes take our waste to treatment plants. There it is treated in three stages:

- Primary treatment simply consists of large tanks that allow solids to settle out.
- Secondary treatment removes organic materials and nutrients. This is done with the help of bacteria – the waste flows to large, aerated tanks where bacteria consume everything they can.
- Typically, tertiary treatment will use chemicals to remove phosphorus and nitrogen from the water, but may also include filter beds and other types of treatment. Chlorine added to the water kills any remaining bacteria, and the water is discharged.

Treated in this way, sewage is made safe. Where this does not happen harmful pollution is likely. Sewage can spread diseases and, with a high BOD (see page 42), can kill fish in rivers.

CUTTING EDGE: FROM TOILET TO TABLE

The island state of Singapore has never been able to collect and store enough water for its population. Now, to help it become more self-sufficient, it is recycling water from sewers into drinking water. The sewage water is purified in a three-stage process of micro-filtration, reverse **osmosis**, and UV light disinfection.

To launch the product, free bottled samples labelled *NEWwater* were distributed to Singaporeans. It seems as though the idea is spreading. Other parts of the world with water shortages – including California, USA – are planning similar schemes.

Recycling vehicles

A 20-year-old car is now quite an unusual sight – they are normally scrapped and replaced well before that age. What happens to cars when we throw them away? Most of them end up in a scrap yard. There the main material – steel – of the body is recycled. However, a modern car contains thousands of different chemicals, many of which are hazardous. Since 2005, car owners in many countries in Europe have been obliged to take their old cars to registered decontamination centres. There the toxic chemicals in airbags, brake fluid, and metals (such as mercury and lead) are removed safely.

However, this European law is not always obeyed. In Sweden and the Netherlands, 85 percent of old cars have been recycled. In the United Kingdom the figure is only 33 percent and an estimated 1.3 million cars were dumped illegally in 2006.

Pollute or protect?

Car tyres eventually wear thin and have to be replaced. Where do the old tyres go? In Europe, all used tyres now have to be recycled. In other parts of the world they have been put to a novel use. Thousands of old tyres have been tied together and sunk in the sea to create artificial reefs. The tyres become covered in seaweed and are an ideal shape to provide a home and breeding ground for fish, crabs, and lobsters. Is this a good way of protecting sea creatures, or is it another form of pollution?

Although it is artificial, this reef made of tyres is providing a home for a variety of sea creatures.

Plastic problems

In the modern world you cannot escape from plastics. Just have a look around at home and count the plastic items you can see. Unfortunately, the properties of plastics that make them useful – they are cheap, durable, and long-lasting – mean that they are not easy to get rid of. We can't go to many places now without finding some plastic litter.

There are two main problems with plastic. Firstly, they do not break down easily in the environment and, secondly, it is not always easy to recycle them. The problem is that plastics must be sorted before they are recycled and many authorities do not provide adequate sorting facilities. However, it can be done. Accurate figures are hard to establish, but, for example, the United States claims to recycle 40 percent of its containers and packaging.

IN YOUR HOME: PLASTICS

In 1988, plastics manufacturers agreed a labelling system to help people recycle different types of plastic. Look on bottles and packaging materials for the recycling triangle. In the centre of it you will find a number. This number identifies the type of plastic. Some plastics can be recycled more easily than others. Plastic numbers 1, 2, and 3 are the easiest to recycle.

Water bottles are made from a plastic called polyethylene terephthalate (PET), which can easily be recycled. In Switzerland and Germany there is an extra cost on bottled drinks, which can be reclaimed when the bottle is recycled.

Midway Island

The coral atoll of Midway was the site of a famous World War II battle. Now it is the scene of a battle against pollution. Situated in the Pacific Ocean, Midway is home to some of the world's most endangered species and they are at risk from the vast amount of plastic waste drifting in the ocean.

Two million albatrosses live on Midway. Scientists have come to the staggering conclusion that every one of them contains some quantity of plastic. Albatrosses live on seafood, such as squid. To an albatross, some of the floating pieces of plastic – like disposable cigarette lighters – look very much like food. Adult birds will even, unknowingly, feed plastic to their offspring. Some of the albatrosses on Midway are never able to fly due to the weight of plastic in their stomachs. Others choke to death on plastic, or starve to death because their stomachs are full of indigestible plastic objects, such as deodorant sticks or carrier bags. Typically, a dead albatross from Midway might contain the handle of a toothbrush, a bottle top, and a piece of fishing net! Wildlife officers on the island do their best to tackle the problem. But the problem is global. The situation on Midway is caused by the vast amount of cheap plastic goods that are designed to be disposable.

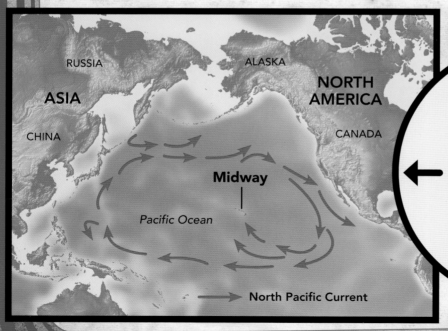

It is estimated that about 100 tonnes of "plastic soup" is circulating in the North Pacific, covering an area about twice the size of the United States. Currents circulating in the Pacific Ocean bring floating rubbish – mainly plastic – to Midway.

Pacific currents continue to collect plastic and other rubbish on Midway putting albatrosses, like this Laysan, at risk.

Tantalum and gorillas

Mobile phones are amazing pieces of technology containing advanced electronic systems. The metal tantalum is used to store electrical charge in a phone. It is a completely safe metal – much better to use than others, such as toxic lead or cadmium. However, where does tantalum come from? Tantalum is mined in forests in the Congo basin area in Africa – the home of the rare mountain gorilla. The invasion of miners to obtain tantalum ore has led to gorillas being killed for food and their habitat has been reduced.

Recycling computers

Thirty million computers are thrown out each year in the United States alone. Most will be sent for recycling, but what actually happens to them? Recycling companies have found they can make more money by sending old PCs to India. There, people work for about 25p a day to reclaim valuable, reusable metals from old PCs. However, computers contain many hazardous chemicals, such as mercury, lead, and POPs. Some of these are just dumped. Others are burnt and release poisons. This recycling process is both hazardous to the workers and damaging to the environment.

And finally...

This book has described some of the successes achieved in the fight against pollution and some of the challenges that remain. Green Chemistry (see page 41) encourages us to look at the whole lifespan of our goods and chemicals. Where do they come from and where do they end up? Is the whole process sustainable? The two examples above show that what seems to be environmentally sound might not be quite as good as we first thought.

Facts and figures

The world's most polluted places

The table below shows some of the world's most polluted places, and the reasons for that pollution.

Place, Country	Type of pollution	Cause of pollution	Number of people affected
Sumgayit, Azerbaijan	Organic chemicals, oil, and heavy metals (including mercury)	Petrochemical and industrial complexes	275,000
Linfen, China	Ash, carbon monoxide, nitrogen oxides, PM-2.5, PM-10, sulfur dioxide, volatile organic compounds, arsenic, lead	Automobile and industrial emissions	3,000,000
Tianying, China	Lead and other heavy metals	Mining and processing	140,000
Sukinda, India	Hexavalent chromium and other metals	Chromite mines and processing	2,600,000
Vapi, India	Chemicals and heavy metals	Industrial estates	71,000
La Oroya, Peru	Lead, copper, zinc, and sulfur dioxide	Heavy metal mining and processing	35,000
Dzerzhinsk, Russia	Chemicals and toxic by-products – including Sarin, VX gas, and also lead and phenols	Cold War-era chemical weapons manufacturing	300,000
Norilsk, Russia	Air pollution – particulates, sulfur dioxide, heavy metals (nickel, copper, cobalt, lead, selenium), phenols, hydrogen sulphide	Major nickel and related metals mining and processing	134,000
Chernobyl, Ukraine	Radioactive dust – including uranium, plutonium, cesium-137, strontium, and other metals	Meltdown of reactor core in 1986	Initially 5.5 million, now disputed numbers
Kabwe, Zambia	Lead, cadmium	Lead mining and processing	255,000

Source: List compiled in 2007 by the Blacksmith Institute, a leading U.S. organization that supports pollution projects.

Steps to success

It's not all doom and gloom! Countries around the world are fighting pollution. The table below shows some ways they are tackling it.

Location	Action
Santiago, Chile	Moving faster than any country in Latin America, Chile is accelerating the introduction of ultra-low sulfur fuels and much cleaner vehicles in metropolitan Santiago, where air pollution challenges are toughest.
Beijing, China	China's top environmental official claimed that China is aiming to reduce its emissions of sulfur dioxide significantly as it steps up efforts to fight pollution.
Chesapeake Bay, USA	The largest and most productive estuary in the USA suffered badly from eutrophication. In 1987, measures were taken to reduce the nutrient run-off into the bay. While pollution levels have dropped, challenges remain.
Scotland, UK	Scotland has set the toughest targets in the UK for the reduction of air pollution levels over the next decade. Expect to see an overall reduction in its air pollution of more than 50 percent by 2010.
Mexico City, Mexico	Renowned for its air pollution problems, Mexico City has identified over 85 air pollution and greenhouse gas emissions reduction actions to be implemented over an eight-year period from 2004.
Canberra, Australia	Former Australian Minister for the Environment and Heritage, Ian Campbell, committed AUS$3 million in government funding to support a local initiative encouraging communities and individuals to walk, cycle, use public transport, and limit the use of private vehicles.
Tokyo, Japan	As Japan strives to cut its greenhouse gas emissions to meet Kyoto Protocol targets, solar cell makers are increasing their sales.
Turin, Italy	A car company recently announced that it is teaming up with the Italian Ministry for the Environment and the country's oil industry in a new drive to promote low-emission, methane-powered vehicles and reduce air pollution in Italy's cities.
Bangkok, Thailand	Thailand's national gas and oil company pledged to reduce air pollution and toxic waste from their main industrial complex in the east of the country.
Manila, Philippines	Millions of tonnes of oil and waste quietly end up in waters around the Philippines every year, as a result of either accidental or occupational pollution. A proposal for harsher penalties for unlawful dumping of waste materials in territorial seas is now pending before the country's government.

Biographies

Rachel Carson (1907–1964)

Growing up in rural Pennsylvania, USA, Rachel Carson developed a life-long love of nature that she expressed as a writer and marine biologist. In 1952, she published her prize-winning study of the ocean, *The Sea Around Us* (1951), which was followed by *The Edge of the Sea* in 1955. These books made Carson famous as a naturalist and science writer. Disturbed by the use of pesticides, Carson changed her focus in order to warn about the effects of misusing these chemicals. In *Silent Spring* (1962), she challenged scientists and the government by calling for a change in the way humans viewed the natural world. Carson was attacked as an alarmist. Even so, she courageously spoke out to remind us that we are a part of the natural world and subject to the same damage as the rest of the ecosystem. Rachel Carson died in 1964, after a long battle against breast cancer.

Ma Jun (born 1969)

In 2008, *The Guardian* (a leading British newspaper) selected Chinese environmentalist Ma Jun as one of 50 people who could save the planet. This was because of his green efforts in the past decade. Ma Jun created a website to name and shame Chinese companies, and even local governments, that pollute the environment. *"Companies which may ignore fines or other punishments cannot afford their brands being blacklisted"*, he said. In 2006, Ma Jun set up the Institute of Public and Environmental Affairs, a Beijing-based, non-governmental organization.

James Lovelock (born 1919)

Inventor James Lovelock worked as a research scientist in London and at Harvard University in the United States before establishing himself as an independent scientist. While working for NASA on space probes to be sent to Mars, Lovelock became interested in the Martian atmosphere. Comparing it to the atmosphere on Earth, he developed a theory – which he named the Gaia Hypothesis, after a Greek goddess. Lovelock's theory states that the living and non-living parts of Earth form a complex system that can be thought of as a living organism. Many environmentalists have welcomed Lovelock's views that all living things affect Earth's environment, which, in turn, promotes life overall. Lovelock believes that Earth will in time heal itself, but environmental disaster is inevitable. Not all scientists accept the Gaia Hypothesis or Lovelock's predictions.

Thomas Midgley (1889–1944)

Thomas Midgley was a U.S. chemist and his first success, in 1921, was to find a chemical that improved the efficiency of petrol. Soon all oil companies were adding lead tetraethyl to their fuel. In 1930, came his discovery of CFCs as a safe refrigerant in fridges. While praised at the time for his discoveries, today we are more critical considering the serious negative environmental impacts they have had. One historian remarked that Midgley *"had more impact on the atmosphere than any other single organism in Earth's history"*. In later life, Midgley became disabled through polio. He set up an elaborate rig of ropes and pulleys to lift him from his bed. Unfortunately, he became entangled in the ropes and died of strangulation.

Mario Molina (born 1943)

The son of a Mexican lawyer and diplomat, Mario Molina chose to study chemistry. After obtaining a degree he went into research. With his colleague, F. Sherwood Rowland, he found evidence that CFCs might be damaging the ozone layer in the atmosphere. Few people showed any interest so Molina and Rowland staged a press conference in Atlanta in 1974. It was another two years before supporting evidence was accepted. As a result, the worldwide elimination of CFCs and the Montreal Protocol on protecting the ozone layer were put in place. Molina and Rowland shared the 1995 Nobel Prize in Chemistry. Molina remains the first and only Mexican to receive a Nobel Prize for science.

Patrick Moore (born 1947)

While studying life sciences at the University of British Columbia in Canada, Moore became inspired by ecology – the science of how all living things are interconnected. When he saw the effects of human, industrial, nuclear, and other pollution, it moved him to engage in environmental activism. This resulted in him co-founding the environment campaign group Greenpeace with several other people. Dr Moore is no longer a member of Greenpeace, but he is still passionate and outspoken about the environment.

Find out more

Books

Global Warming, Ron Fridell (Franklin Watts, 2007)

Planet Under Pressure: Pollution, Clive Gifford (Raintree, 2006)

Science at the Edge: Alternative Energy Sources, Sally Morgan (Heinemann, 2009)

Silent Spring, Rachel Carson (Penguin Modern Classics, 2000)

What Do You Think? Can Earth Support Our Growing Population?, Kate Shuster (Heinemann, 2009)

Websites

- http://news.bbc.co.uk/1/hi/programmes/bhopal/default.stm
  Learn about one of the world's worst industrial disasters that happened in Bhopal, India, in 1984.

- http://science.howstuffworks.com/cleaning-oil-spill.htm
  Find out more about cleaning up oil pollution.

- http://www.lbl.gov/Education/ELSI/pollution-main.html
  Find out about air pollution, including inside your home.

- http://www.ace.mmu.ac.uk/eae/air_quality/air_quality.html
  A comprehensive list of all things related to air pollution.

- http://www.ec.gc.ca/acidrain/
  Canada is a country that has suffered badly from acid rain. This site tells the whole story of acid rain.

- http://www.foei.org/
  Friends of the Earth is the world's largest environmental network with members in 70 countries.

- http://www.greenpeace.org/international/
  Greenpeace is a well-known international group committed to
  protecting the environment.

- http://www.carbontrust.co.uk
  The Carbon Trust is a UK organization that helps individuals
  and businesses reduce their carbon footprint.

- http://www.howstuffworks.com/nuclear-power.htm
  Learn more about nuclear power and the radioactive materials
  needed to generate it.

- http://www.world-nuclear.org/education/wast.htm
  Read about the ins and outs of nuclear waste.

- http://www.recyclenow.com/
  Packed with all you'll need to know about recycling near you.

- http://ozonewatch.gsfc.nasa.gov/
  Check on the status of the ozone layer over the South Pole.

Topics for further research

- Research the *Exxon Valdez* disaster. What is the situation now
  on the coast where the spill occurred?

- The Chinese government closed many factories in an attempt
  to lessen pollution before the summer Olympic Games in 2008.
  Have the improvements in air quality been maintained?

Glossary

acid rain   rain (or snow or hail) that is unusually acidic. Normal rain is naturally very slightly acidic. Acid rain has a lower pH than normal.

algae   (singular alga) large group of simple, plant-like organisms

bioaccumulation   when an organism absorbs a toxic substance at a rate greater than that at which the substance is lost. The amount of the chemical therefore increases in the organism.

biodegradable   material that can be naturally broken down by bacteria

bioindicator   organism or chemical used to monitor the health of the environment

carbon footprint   measure of the impact that human activities have on the environment in terms of the amount of carbon dioxide produced

catalyst   substance that will speed up a chemical reaction without being used up itself

deforestation   clearing of an area of forest or trees

DNA (deoxyribonucleic acid)   molecules in all organisms that carry genetic information

ecosystem   system of plants, animals, and micro-organisms that live together in a particular environment

enzyme   complex molecules that control reactions within cells

eutrophication   increase in chemical nutrients in part of the environment. The term is often used to mean the increase in plant growth and decay, the consequent lack of oxygen, and severe reductions in water quality, and numbers of fish and other aquatic animals.

fossil fuel   coal, oil, or natural gas that originated millions of years ago

genetic modification   artificially altering the genetic make up to produce a certain characteristic

greenhouse gas   gas present in the atmosphere, which reduces the loss of heat into space and contributes to increasing global temperatures

groundwater   water found below the surface in porous soil and cracks in rocks

incinerated   burned

industrialized   containing many industries

infrared   radiation that is not visible, but is emitted by hot objects

moderator   in a nuclear reactor it is the material that slows neutrons down

nuclear fission   splitting of the nucleus of an atom into two parts

nutrient   substance that an organism uses to grow, which must be taken in from the environment

organic   describes material that has recently come from a living organism. In chemistry, organic describes compounds based on the element carbon.

osmosis   where molecules from a less concentrate solution pass through a semipermeable membrane to a more concentrate solution

ozone   form of oxygen with three atoms (O_3) joined in a molecule. At ground level it is a pollutant, but in the upper atmosphere it protects against dangerous radiation.

pesticide   substance used for preventing, controlling, or lessening the damage caused by a pest

pH   scale to show how acid or alkaline a substance is: 7 is neutral, lower than 7 is more acidic, higher is more alkaline

pharmaceutical   to do with the preparation or sale of medicinal drugs

photosynthesis   conversion of light energy into chemical energy by plants

radioactive   describes a substance in which the atoms decay and emit radiation (energy and other particles)

renewable   natural resources (materials or energy) that can be replenished as quickly as they are used up

slag heap   a pile of waste from coal mining

smog   a mixture of smoke and fog

sustainable   describes resources that can be maintained at current levels indefinitely

toxic   describes substances that are harmful to living things

ultraviolet   (UV) high-energy radiation that is not visible. Emitted naturally from the Sun, it causes sunburn and other harmful effects.

Index